FROM STARTUP TO SCALE-UP

The Ultimate Guide to Accelerating Your Business Growth, Discover the Key Attributes and Mindsets That Propel Entrepreneurs to the Top

Ricardo B. Salls

CONTENTS

INTRODUCTION

Embarking on an entrepreneurial trip to start a successful business is an adventure that blends ambition, creativity, and strategic thinking. Whether you are driven by a groundbreaking idea, a passion for a particular assiduity, or the desire to chart your professional course, the path to success requires careful planning and deliberate conduct. In this companion, we'll explore the crucial rudiments and ways necessary to not only launch a business but also to cultivate a terrain where it can thrive.

At the heart of any successful business is a compelling conception that addresses a need or solves a problem. We will claw into the process of creativity and how to upgrade your vision, ensuring it aligns with request demands. From there, we'll guide you through the essential way of creating a robust business plan — one that serves as a roadmap, outlining your pretensions, target followership, profit aqueducts, and functional strategies.

Navigating the complications of enrollment, securing backing, and understanding legal conditions is a critical phase in laying the roots for your adventure. This companion will clarify these processes, furnishing practical perceptivity to help you establish a strong foundation for your business.

In the ever-evolving geography of entrepreneurship, effective marketing is crucial to erecting brand mindfulness and connecting with your followership. We will explore innovative marketing strategies and digital tools that can elevate your business's visibility in a competitive request.

Beyond the logistics, we'll claw into the entrepreneurial mindset and the rates that contribute to success. From embracing calculated pitfalls to fostering adaptability and rigidity, developing these characteristics is pivotal for prostrating challenges and sustaining long-term growth.

Starting a successful business isn't just about fiscal earnings — it's about creating value, making a meaningful impact, and contributing to the larger business ecosystem. Join us on this trip as we navigate the way, strategies, and mindset needed to turn your entrepreneurial vision into a thriving and sustainable reality.

CHAPTER ONE
LAYING THE FOUNDATION FOR SUCCESS
Decoding the Startup Ecosystem

Have you ever pictured creating a commodity from scratch, turning your brilliant ideas into a thriving business that makes a real impact? Drink to the stirring world of startups, where passion meets invention and dreams take flight. But before diving headfirst into this dynamic realm, you need to unleash the secrets of the incipiency ecosystem, where dreams are nurtured and businesses are born.

- decrypting the Startup Ecosystem is your ultimate companion to becoming a smart entrepreneur, ready to navigate the challenges and seize the openings. You will embark on an entrepreneurial adventure to

- Unravel the mystifications of the incipiency world, understanding the players, places, and dynamics that drive it forward

- Craft a compelling business plan, your roadmap to success, outlining your vision, charge, and strategy

- Assemble a dream platoon, the hustler behind your incipiency's growth, chancing the right people with the right chops

7

- Uncover retired request gems, the energy for your incipiency's expansion, relating unmet requirements and untapped implicit

- Develop a strategic growth playbook, your design for conquering the request, outlining your path to palm

- Optimize operations and coffers, icing your incipiency can gauge with ease, laying the foundation for sustainable growth

- Cultivate invention, the lifeblood of sustainable success, embracing creativity and trial to stay ahead of the wind

- figure brand fidelity, the foundation of enduring client connections, creating a brand that resonates and guests adore

- Navigate the competitive geography, arising victorious from the business battleground, overreaching your rivals

- Plan for successful exits, maximizing the value of your entrepreneurial trip, icing a satisfying outgrowth

The incipiency ecosystem is a vibrant and ever-evolving geography brimming with ambitious entrepreneurs chasing their dreams of transforming groundbreaking ideas into reality. Embarking on the incipiency trip is an exhilarating yet grueling bid, taking a mix of passion, perseverance, and strategic planning to successfully navigate the intricate phases of the incipiency lifecycle.

The Startup Lifecycle A Roadmap for Entrepreneurial Success

The incipiency lifecycle can be astronomically divided into five distinct stages, each with its own set of challenges and openings

1. creativity and confirmation

The birth of every incipiency lies in a compelling idea that addresses an unmet request need or solves a pressing problem. This original stage involves rigorous request exploration to validate the idea's viability, assess its implicit impact, and upgrade it into a palpable conception.

2. launching and Planning

With a validated idea, the entrepreneur assembles a founding platoon, a different group of individualities with reciprocal chops and movies, to bring the vision to life. This stage also involves establishing the legal structure of the company, developing a comprehensive business plan, and securing the necessary backing to fuel the adventure's growth.

3. Launching and Growth

The adventure officially launches, marking the transition from planning to prosecution. The focus shifts to acquiring guests, erecting brand mindfulness, and generating profit. The company establishes operations, manages force, and tools effective marketing juggernauts to reach its target followership.

4. Expansion and Maturity

As the company gains growth, it expands its request reach, develops new products or services, and enhances its functional effectiveness. The focus shifts to spanning the business, erecting a strong commercial culture, and attracting strategic hookups to fuel further growth.

5. Exit and Beyond

The incipiency may pursue colorful exit strategies, similar to accessions, combinations, original public immolations(IPOs), or operation buyouts. These strategies give entrepreneurs fiscal prices and the occasion to pursue new gambles or contribute to the entrepreneurial ecosystem.

Navigating Challenges and Embracing Openings

The incipiency trip isn't without its hurdles. Entrepreneurs face a multitude of obstacles, such as securing backing, attracting top gifts, managing growth, and conforming to dynamic request conditions. still, these challenges also present openings for invention, literacy, and adaptability.

Essential Strategies for Startup Success

Embrace client Centricity

Continuously gather feedback, dissect client geste, and acclimatize your products or services to meet their evolving requirements.

make a Strong platoon

compass yourself with talented individuals who partake in your vision, retain the necessary chops, and round your moxie. Foster a cooperative and probative work terrain to maximize platoon performance.

Adaptive and Agile Approach

Be set to pivot and acclimatize your strategies as request conditions change, new challenges crop, and unlooked-for challenges arise. Embrace invention and trial to stay ahead of the wind.

Effective Financial Management

Prudently manage your finances to ensure sustainable growth. Seek professional guidance on investment openings, fiscal planning, and managing cash inflow to optimize resource allocation.

Seek Mentorship and Support

influence the knowledge and experience of instructors, counselors, and assiduity experts. share in incipiency communities and networks to gain precious perceptivity, connect with implicit mates, and admit support from fellow entrepreneurs.

Beyond the Startup Lifecycle nonstop literacy and Growth

The incipiency trip does not end with an exit; it's an ongoing process of literacy, growth, and donation to the broader entrepreneurial ecosystem. Successful entrepreneurs continue to introduce and explore new gambles, share their knowledge and experience with others, and inspire the coming generation of disruptive startups.

A well-drafted business plan serves as your compass, guiding you through the uncharted waters of entrepreneurship. It's not just a formality; it's a living document that articulates your vision, outlines your strategy, and attracts the coffers you need to transfigure your idea into a thriving business.

Why Craft a Compelling Business Plan?

A compelling business plan serves multiple purposes

- Clarity and concentration, It forces you to easily define your business pretensions, target requests, and competitive geography, furnishing a roadmap for your entrepreneurial trip.

- Investor magnet Implicit investors seek a structured plan that demonstrates your understanding of the request, your capability to execute, and the eventuality for fiscal returns.

- Internal Alignment It aligns your platoon with a participated vision and strategy, ensuring everyone is on the same runner as you navigate challenges and make opinions.

The substance of a Compelling Business Plan

A compelling business plan isn't a lengthy, slang-filled document; it's a terse, conclusive narrative that captures the substance of your business. It should be acclimatized to your specific followership, whether it's implicit investors, mates, or indeed your platoon.

Key Components of a Compelling Business Plan

Administrative Summary The terse elevator pitch of your business, pressing the problem you break, your unique value proposition, and your target request.

Company Description A detailed overview of your company, its history, charge, vision, and values, furnishing environment for your business adventure.

request Analysis A thorough understanding of your target request, including demographics, trends, and competitive geography, demonstrating your grasp of the assiduity.

Product or Service Description A comprehensive explanation of your product or service, its unique features, and how it addresses client requirements, showcasing your invention.

Marketing and Deals Strategy A detailed plan for reaching your target request, pricing your product or service, and generating deals, demonstrating your understanding of client accession.

operation platoon An preface to your crucial platoon members, pressing their moxie and experience, showcasing the gift behind your adventure.

fiscal protrusions A realistic cast of your profit, charges, and profitability, demonstrating your fiscal wit and understanding of the business model.

Casting a Compelling Business Plan Tips for Success

❖ Start Beforehand Begin casting your business plan beforehand, as it'll evolve as your business grows.

❖ Be Clear and Concise Use plain language, avoid slang, and concentrate on the most important information.

❖ Tell a Compelling Story Engage your followership with a narrative that captures the substance of your business.

❖ punctuate Your Oneness Emphasize what makes your business stand out from the competition.

❖ Seek Feedback Partake your plan with instructors, counsels, or implicit investors to gather precious perceptivity.

Flashback, your business plan is a dynamic document that should be redefined and streamlined regularly as your business grows and evolves. It's your roadmap to success, so treat it with the care and attention it deserves

Assembling a Winning Team, The Power of People

In the dynamic world of startups, your platoon is your most precious asset. They're the ones who breathe life into your ideas, turn your vision into reality, and propel your incipiency towards success. Assembling a winning platoon isn't just about hiring the right people; it's about creating a cohesive unit, a symphony of different bents working in perfect harmony to achieve a common thing.

Why is a Winning Team Crucial?

A winning platoon is the driving force behind every successful incipiency. They

- **Bring Different Chops and Perspectives** A blend of moxie, backgrounds, and shoes enriches the decision-making process and fosters creativity.

- **Partake a Common Vision and Passion** A participated sense of purpose and enthusiasm energies provocation and drives the platoon to achieve common pretensions.

- **Embrace Collaboration and Communication** Open communication, an amenability to unite, and a culture of collective respect produce a positive and productive work terrain.

16

- **Demonstrate dexterity and Rigidity** The capability to acclimatize to changing request conditions, embrace new technologies, and pivot when necessary is essential for long-term success.

Assembling Your Winning Team Strategies for Success

1. **Identify the crucial places** Determine the essential places demanded to support your incipiency's growth, from specialized experts to marketing wizards and deals exponents.

2. **Seek Out the Right Fit** Look for individuals who not only retain the needed chops but also align with your company culture and partake in your vision for the future.

3. **Emphasize Cultural Fit** A strong company culture fosters a sense of belonging, encourages collaboration, and attracts top gifts who partake in your values.

4. **Embrace Diversity** A different platoon brings a wealth of perspectives, gests, and problem-working approaches, leading to invention and better decision- timber.

5. **Invest in Training and Development** Continuously invest in your platoon's professional growth through training, mentorship, and openings for skill development.

6. **Nurture a Culture of Feedback** Encourage open and formative feedback, allowing individuals to learn, grow, and contribute effectively.

7. **Celebrate Successes and Fete** Achievements Acknowledge and celebrate your platoon's accomplishments, fostering a positive and motivating work terrain. your platoon is the foundation upon which your incipiency's success is erected. By precisely assembling, nurturing, and empowering your platoon, you set your incipiency on a line for sustainable growth and lasting impact.

CHAPTER TWO
FROM IDEA TO IMPACT
Identifying Growth Opportunities for Your Startup

In the dynamic world of startups, growth is the lifeblood of success. relating untapped request openings is like uncovering retired treasures, furnishing your incipiency with the energy it needs to expand its reach, increase its profit, and achieve its full eventuality.

Why is relating Growth openings Crucial?

Unveiling retired request openings offers several advantages for your incipiency

- o **Fueling Expansion** Discovering untapped requests allows you to expand your client base, adding deals and profit.

- o **Enhancing Competitive Advantage** relating unique request niches can separate your incipiency from challengers, furnishing a strategic edge.

- o **Driving Innovation** Understanding rising client requirements and untapped eventualities can spark an invention, leading to new product or service immolations.

- o **Securing Funding** Investors are attracted to startups that demonstrate a clear path to growth and untapped request eventuality.

Strategies for relating Growth openings

i. **dissect Market Trends** Stay acquainted with rising trends, evolving consumer actions, and shifting assiduity dynamics to identify implicit growth areas.

ii. **Conduct Competitor Analysis** Completely dissect your challengers' strengths, and sins, and request positioning to uncover openings they may have overlooked.

iii. **Engage with guests** Gather direct feedback from your guests to understand their unmet requirements, preferences, and pain points, which can lead to untapped request openings.

iv. **Explore Unconventional Channels** Venture beyond traditional request exploration styles and explore unconventional channels, similar to social media, online forums, and assiduity events, to uncover retired request gems.

v. **Embrace Innovation** Encourage a culture of creativity and trial within your platoon to induce innovative ideas that address arising request requirements.
- o **Seek External moxie** Consult with assiduity experts, request judges, and business advisers to gain perceptivity into arising trends and implicit growth openings. relating growth openings is an ongoing process that requires nonstop exploration, request analysis, and client engagement. By laboriously seeking out retired request gems, you place your incipiency for sustainable growth and long-term success.

Your Startup's GPS to Sustainable Growth

Having a clear and well-defined strategic roadmap is akin to enjoying a sophisticated GPS guiding you toward your destination. It serves as a comprehensive design that outlines your incipiency's pretensions, strategies, and the strictly drafted way you will take to achieve them, ensuring you stay focused and on track as you navigate the ever-changing entrepreneurial geography.

The foundation of Success Why a Strategic Roadmap is pivotal

A strategic roadmap isn't simply a document; it's the foundation upon which your incipiency's success is erected. It provides a plethora of benefits that propel your adventure towards sustainable growth

Clarity and Direction: it easily defines your incipiency's vision, charge, and pretensions, furnishing your platoon with a participated sense of purpose and direction, ensuring everyone is rowing in the same direction.

Alignment and concentration: It align your platoon's sweats and coffers towards achieving common objectives, ensuring everyone is working towards the same thing, barring haphazard sweats and maximizing impact.

Informed Decision-Making: It serves as a frame for forming informed opinions, guiding your strategies and conduct, and ensuring your choices aren't grounded on guesswork or freakishness.

Responsibility and Progress Tracking: It establishes clear mileposts and timelines, fostering responsibility and ensuring progress is tracked, keeping your adventure on the right line.

Investor Confidence and Partnership: It demonstrates your incipiency's focus, credibility, and implicit for growth, attracting investors and mates who can fuel your success, furnishing both fiscal support and strategic guidance.

Developing Your Strategic Roadmap, A Step- by- Step by-Step Companion to Navigating the Entrepreneurial Maze

Casting a strategic roadmap isn't a one-time bid; it's an ongoing process that requires careful consideration, strategic planning, and nonstop adaption. Then is a step-by-step companion to navigating the entrepreneurial maze and casting a roadmap that paves the way for success

1. Defining Your Vision, Mission, and Values Begin by articulating your incipiency's core purpose, its reason for actuality, and the guiding principles that will shape its opinions and conduct. Your vision should be audacious and inspiring, while your charge should be terse and easily define the problem you're working on.

2. Establishing Clear Pretensions Set specific, measurable, attainable, applicable, and time-bound (SMART) pretensions that align with your vision and charge. These pretensions should be challenging yet attainable, furnishing a sense of direction and achievement as you progress.

3. assaying Your Current Position Conduct, a thorough assessment of your incipiency's current strengths, sins, openings, and pitfalls (geek analysis) to understand your internal capabilities and external terrain. This analysis

provides pivotal perceptivity into your competitive edge and areas that bear enhancement.

4. relating Strategic enterprise Determine the crucial enterprise that will help you achieve your pretensions, considering factors similar as request eventuality, competitive geography, and resource vacuity. This enterprise should be innovative, poignant, and aligned with your overall strategy.

5. Developing an Action Plan produces a detailed action plan that outlines the specific way, timelines, and coffers needed for each action. This action plan should be broken down into manageable tasks, icing clarity and responsibility.

6. Communicating and Aligning easily communicate your strategic roadmap to your platoon, ensuring everyone understands their places, liabilities, and benefactions. This alignment fosters a sense of power and motivates individuals to contribute their stylish.

7. Monitoring and conforming Regularly cover progress, estimate performance against your pretensions, and make adaptations as demanded to acclimatize to changing request conditions or challenges. This nonstop monitoring ensures your roadmap remains applicable and effective. a

strategic roadmap isn't a static document; it's an evolving companion that should be redefined and streamlined regularly as your incipiency grows, the business terrain changes, and new openings crop.

where invention and dexterity reign supreme, casting a compelling strategy is just the first step on the path to success. The true test falsehoods in rephrasing that strategy into palpable results, transubstantiating grand fancies into a thriving reality. This process of strategy prosecution is the ground that connects dreams to reality, where ideas are converted into poignant conduct and bourns are moldered into concrete achievements.

The Challenge of Strategy Prosecution

The gap between strategy expression and prosecution is frequently undervalued. While creating a well-defined strategy is pivotal, it's the effective prosecution of that strategy that determines the ultimate success or failure of an incipiency.

The challenges of strategy prosecution stem from colorful factors

Aligning brigades and coffers: ensures that all platoon members understand the strategy, are aligned with the pretensions, and have the necessary coffers to execute their places effectively.

prostrating Organizational Inertia: Breaking down silos, fostering a culture of collaboration, and conforming to change can be delicate within established associations.

conforming to Market Dynamics: The capability to acclimatize strategies to changing request conditions, client preferences, and technological advancements is essential for long-term success.

Strategies for Effective Strategy Prosecution

Bridging the gap between strategy and prosecution requires a combination of strategic planning, organizational alignment, and nonstop adaption. Then are some crucial strategies to effectively turn your incipiency strategy into reality

Establish Clear Goals and Metrics

easily define measurable pretensions and objects that align with your overall strategy. Establish criteria to track progress and measure the effectiveness of your prosecution sweats.

Communicate Effectively

easily communicate your strategy to your platoon, ensuring everyone understands their places, liabilities, and how their work contributes to the overall pretensions.

Empower Your Team

Fosters a culture of power and commission, giving your platoon the autonomy to form opinions and take action within their areas of moxie.

Align coffers and Processes

ensure that your platoon has the necessary coffers, tools, and processes to execute the strategy effectively. Streamline processes and exclude inefficiencies that hamper progress.

Embrace nonstop enhancement

Continuously cover progress, estimate performance, and make adaptations to your strategy as demanded to acclimatize to changing request conditions and challenges.

Turning strategy into reality is a nonstop trip, not a one-time event. By enforcing these strategies, you can empower your incipiency to ground the gap between vision and prosecution, transforming your dreams into a thriving reality.

CHAPTER THREE

FUELING GROWTH UNLEASHING THE POTENTIAL OF YOUR STARTUP

Growth is the lifeblood of success. It's the driving force that propels your adventure from a rookie idea into a thriving enterprise, transforming your vision into a palpable reality. Fueling growth isn't just about adding profit or expanding your client base; it's about unleashing the untapped eventuality within your incipiency, unleashing a swell of invention, effectiveness, and client satisfaction that propels you towards sustainable growth and lasting impact.

Why is Fueling Growth important?

Fueling growth is essential for your incipiency's success because it

Expands Market Reach

Growth allows you to reach a wider followership, adding your client base and profit eventuality.

Enhances Competitive Advantage

Sustained growth strengthens your request position, securing you from challengers and attracting investors.

Drives Innovation and Adaptability

The pursuit of growth fosters a culture of invention and dexterity, enabling you to acclimatize to changing request dynamics and evolving client requirements.

Attracts Talent and Coffers

Growth attracts top gifts and coffers, fueling your capability to execute your strategies and achieve your pretensions.

Strategies for Fueling Growth

Identify Growth openings

Continuously seek out and dissect untapped request openings, arising trends, and unmet client needs to identify implicit growth areas.

upgrade Your Value Proposition

ensures your value proposition is clear, compelling, and discerned, effectively communicating the benefits your incipiency offers to its target guests.

Optimize Marketing and Deals

Enhance your marketing and deals strategies to reach wider followership, induce leads, and convert them into pious guests.

Embrace Innovation

Cultivate a culture of invention, encouraging trial and threat-taking to develop new products, services, or business models that drive growth.

Streamline Operations

Optimize your operations to enhance effectiveness, reduce costs, and ameliorate client satisfaction, freeing up coffers for growth enterprise.

Seek Backing and Investment

Explore backing options, similar to adventure capital, angel investors, or crowdfunding, to fuel your growth plans and expansion strategies.

Nurture gifts and figure Strong brigades

Invest in the development and retention of top gifts, erecting cohesive brigades that partake in your vision and contribute to your growth line.

acclimatize to Market Dynamics

Continuously cover request trends, client preferences, and technological advancements, conforming your strategies and immolations to stay ahead of the wind. fueling growth is an ongoing process that requires nonstop trouble, strategic planning, and amenability to acclimatize. By enforcing these strategies, you can unleash the untapped eventuality within your incipiency and propel it towards sustainable growth and lasting success.

Attracting the best in the industry

attracting and retaining top gifts is pivotal for organizational success. Top Gift brings a wealth of moxie, experience, and innovative thinking, enabling companies to stay ahead of the wind and achieve their strategic pretensions.

The Significance of Top Gift

Acquiring the stylish in the assiduity offers multitudinous benefits for associations

1. Enhanced Innovation and Problem-working Top gift brings a fresh perspective, different skill sets, and a proven track record of invention. They contribute to a culture of nonstop enhancement, leading to the development of groundbreaking results and strategic advantages.

2. Elevated Productivity and Performance The Top gift is largely professed, motivated, and committed to excellence. They work efficiently, make sound opinions, and constantly deliver high-quality results, contributing to overall organizational productivity and performance.

3. Strengthened Character and Employer Brand Attracting top gifts enhances a company's character as an employer of choice. This attracts indeed more high-quality individualities, creating a righteous cycle of gift accession and retention.

4. Knowledge participating and Mentorship Top Gift frequently serves as instructors and knowledge- participating capitals within an association. They partake in their moxie with associates, fostering a culture of nonstop literacy and professional development.

Strategies for Attracting Top Gift

Establish a Compelling Employer Brand Develop a strong employer brand that showcases the company's values, culture, and commitment to hand growth. produce a positive and engaging hand experience that attracts and retains top gifts.

- produce a Clear Value Proposition and easily articulate the value proposition for implicit workers, pressing the openings for professional growth, development, and impact. Emphasize the company's commitment to diversity, equity, and addition.

- influence Effective Reclamation Strategies use a multi-channel approach to reclamation, including online job boards, social media platforms, hand referrals, and assiduity events. Target applicable gift pools and knitter your reclamation dispatches to specific places and chops.

- Offer Competitive Compensation and Benefits gives competitive compensation packages that align with assiduity norms and fete the value of a top gift. Offer seductive benefits, similar to health insurance, withdrawal plans, flexible work arrangements, and professional development openings.

- Foster a Culture of Innovation and Growth produce a work terrain that encourages invention, creativity, and nonstop literacy. give openings for workers to develop new chops, take on new challenges, and contribute to the company's growth.

- Empower workers and Fete Achievements Empower workers to take the power of their work and make meaningful benefactions. Fete and appreciate hand achievements, both big and small, to foster a sense of value and provocation.

- Nurture Employee Connections Build strong connections with workers, fostering a sense of community and belonging. Encourage open communication, address enterprises instantly, and give openings for feedback.

Cultivating a Talent Magnet

Attracting and retaining top gifts is an ongoing process that requires a strategic and holistic approach. By establishing a strong employer brand, creating a positive work terrain, offering competitive compensation and benefits, and fostering a culture of invention and growth, associations can cultivate a gift attraction, attracting and retaining the stylish in the assiduity to drive sustainable success.

Optimizing Operations for Growth

optimizing operations isn't just a matter of choice; it's an essential survival strategy. It's the art of transubstantiating your incipiency into a well-waxed machine, able to not only meet the demands of the moment but also span seamlessly to meet the challenges and openings of the hereafter. By optimizing operations, you unleash a treasure trove of benefits that propel your incipiency towards sustainable growth and lasting impact.

Why is Optimizing Operations Crucial?

Optimizing operations isn't a one-time event; it's an ongoing process that requires nonstop trouble, strategic planning, and amenability to acclimatize. Then are some compelling reasons why optimizing operations is pivotal for your incipiency's success

Enhances Efficiency By barring inefficiencies and streamlining processes, you maximize productivity, reduce costs, and free up coffers for growth enterprise. This effectiveness translates into reduced charges, increased profit perimeters, and the capability to invest more in invention and expansion.

Improves client Satisfaction Optimized operations lead to brisk delivery times, bettered product quality, and enhanced client service. Satisfied guests come pious lawyers, spreading positive word-of-mouth and generating reprise business, which is the lifeblood of any successful incipiency.

Enhances Scalability A well-waxed functional frame lays the foundation for flawless scalability, enabling your incipiency to acclimatize to growing demand and request expansion. As your client base expands and your immolations grow, optimized operations ensure that you can handle the increased volume and complexity without compromising quality or effectiveness.

Energies Innovation Optimized operations produce a culture of effectiveness and resourcefulness, freeing up time and energy for invention and the development of new products, services, or business models. When your platoon isn't embrangled down by inefficiencies and detainments, they have the internal space and coffers to explore new ideas, trial with new technologies, and develop groundbreaking results that drive your incipiency forward.

Strategies for Optimizing Operations

Identify Backups Conduct a thorough assessment of your current processes to identify areas of inefficiency, detainments, or waste. This could involve assaying workflows, reviewing client feedback, or conducting time studies to pinpoint specific areas where processes are decelerating or creating gratuitous disunion.

Embrace spare Principles Borrow spare principles, similar to barring waste, streamlining workflows, and nonstop enhancement, to optimize resource application and reduce costs. spare principles emphasize Barrington-value-adding conditioning, fastening on what matters most to your guests, and continuously repeating your processes to achieve maximum effectiveness.

influence Technology utensil applicable technologies, similar as robotization, data analytics, and pall- grounded results, to enhance productivity, ameliorate decision- timber, and streamline operations. Technology can automate repetitious tasks, give real-time perceptivity to your business, and enable collaboration across brigades, and anyhow position.

Empower Your Team Fosters a culture of commission, giving your platoon the autonomy to identify and resolve inefficiencies, driving nonstop enhancement from within. Trust your platoon to suggest results, trial with new approaches, and contribute to the overall optimization process.

Streamline Communication Channels Establish clear and effective communication channels to ensure flawless collaboration, reduce detainments, and minimize misconstructions. Break down silos between departments, encourage open communication, and apply tools that grease real-time communication and information sharing.

Regularize processes and apply standardized processes and procedures to ensure thickness, reduce crimes, and ameliorate overall effectiveness. homogenizing processes help exclude variations, ensure everyone is on the same runner, and minimize the threat of miscalculations.

Measure and dissect Performance Continuously track and dissect functional criteria to identify areas for enhancement, examiner progress, and measure the effectiveness of your optimization sweats. Data-driven decision-timber is pivotal for understanding the impact of your optimization sweats and relating areas where further enhancement is demanded.

optimizing operations is an ongoing trip, not a one-time event. By enforcing these strategies, you can transfigure your incipiency into a well-waxed machine, able to fuel sustainable growth and achieve remarkable success. Embrace a culture of nonstop enhancement, acclimatize to changing request dynamics, and empower your platoon to drive functional excellence, and your incipiency will be deposited to navigate the challenges and seize the openings that lie ahead.

Financial Growth Management

In the dynamic and competitive world of startups, where invention and dexterity are the keys to survival and success, fiscal growth operation isn't just a matter of secretary and profit analysis; it's the lifeblood that nourishes and propels an incipiency towards sustainable growth and lasting impact. fiscal growth operation is the art of aligning fiscal objects with strategic growth enterprise, icing that your incipiency has the coffers to fuel its intentions while maintaining fiscal stability and long-term viability.

The substance of Financial Growth Management

fiscal growth operation encompasses a range of critical aspects that inclusively contribute to the fiscal health and sustainable growth of an incipiency

fiscal Planning and Soothsaying

Developing accurate fiscal protrusions, assaying request trends, and anticipating unborn profit and charges are pivotal for guiding your incipiency's fiscal line. This involves creating detailed fiscal models that incorporate colorful scripts, hypotheticals, and implicit pitfalls to give a comprehensive understanding of your incipiency's fiscal future.

Profitability Analysis

Understanding your incipiency's profit motorists, relating cost reduction openings, and optimizing pricing strategies are essential for maximizing profitability. This involves assaying profit aqueducts, charges, and cost structures to identify areas where profitability can be enhanced without compromising product quality or client satisfaction.

Cash Flow Management

icing a steady inflow of cash to meet functional requirements, managing receivables and payables effectively, and avoiding cash inflow dearth's that can hamper growth are critical for maintaining fiscal stability. This involves enforcing robust cash inflow operation practices, similar to collections strategies, payment schedules, and working capital optimization ways.

Funding Acquisition

relating to and pursuing applicable backing sources, similar to adventure capital, angel investors, or crowdfunding, are essential to fuel growth enterprise and expansion plans. This involves understanding the colorful backing options available, assessing the felicity of each option, and erecting a compelling pitch to attract implicit investors.

Investment Evaluation

Assessing implicit investment openings, assessing pitfalls and returns, and making sound investment opinions that align with your incipiency's strategic pretensions are essential for maximizing the value of your incipiency's capital. This involves conducting thorough due industriousness, understanding the terms and conditions of implicit investments, and aligning investment opinions with your incipiency's long-term objectives.

Strategies for Effective Financial Growth Management

Establish Clear Financial Pretensions

The foundation of effective fiscal growth operation lies in setting specific, measurable, attainable, applicable, and time-bound (SMART) fiscal pretensions that align with your overall growth strategy. These pretensions should be quantifiable and aligned with your incipiency's charge, vision, and overall strategic direction.

Develop a Comprehensive Financial Model

A detailed fiscal model serves as a roadmap for your incipiency's fiscal future. It should incorporate profit protrusions, expenditure vatic nations, cash inflow statements, and balance distance protrusions to give a holistic view of your incipiency's fiscal performance and line.

utensil Strong fiscal Controls

Establishing robust fiscal controls is essential for maintaining fiscal integrity, precluding fraud, and maintaining accurate fiscal records.

This includes internal checkups, budget reviews, threat operation practices, and adherence to account norms.

Examiner and dissect fiscal Performance

nonstop monitoring of crucial fiscal criteria, such as profitability, profit growth, cash inflow, and debt-to-equity rates, is pivotal for relating trends, assessing progress, and making timely adaptations to your fiscal strategies. Regular fiscal reporting and analysis give precious perceptivity to the fiscal health of your incipiency.

Seek Expert Financial Guidance

Engaging endured fiscal counsels or adventure plutocrats can give inestimable moxie, guidance, and support in navigating the complex world of incipiency finance. They can help with fiscal modeling, investment opinions, fundraising strategies, and fiscal threat operations.

Financial Growth Management A nonstop trip of adaption

fiscal growth operation isn't a one-time exercise; it's an ongoing trip that requires nonstop adaption and refinement. As your incipiency grows, evolves, faces new challenges, and seizes new openings, your fiscal strategies must acclimatize consequently. Regular reviews of your fiscal plans, protrusions, and performance are essential to ensure that your fiscal strategy remains aligned with your incipiency's evolving pretensions and request conditions. fiscal growth operation isn't just about figures on a spreadsheet; it's about icing that your incipiency has the fiscal coffers, strategies, and moxie in place to fuel its intentions, achieve long-term success, and produce sustainable value for all stakeholders.

Erecting a scalable foundation isn't just a choice; it's an imperative. It's the foundation upon which sustainable growth, long-term viability, and adaptability against unlooked-for challenges are erected. A scalable foundation ensures that your incipiency can seamlessly acclimatize and thrive amidst ever-changing request dynamics, expanding client bases, and adding demands, without compromising quality, effectiveness, or client satisfaction. It's the capability to handle growth gracefully without succumbing to the pressures of expansion.

The Substance of a Scalable Foundation

A scalable foundation isn't just about technology structure or process robotization; it's a holistic approach that encompasses the veritable fabric of your incipiency, from its technological backbone to its organizational culture. It's about designing systems, processes, and structures that can acclimatize and gauge in tandem with your incipiency's growth, icing that your adventure remains nimble, effective, and flexible in the face of change.

The Pillars of a Scalable Foundation

Technology structure

A robust and flexible technology structure forms the bedrock of a scalable incipiency. It should be suitable to handle adding data volumes, stoner business, and new functionalities without performance backups or scalability constraints. Investing in pall-grounded results can give the plainness and scalability demanded to accommodate growth without significant outspoken investments.

Modular and Reusable Architecture

Designing your systems with modularity and reusability in mind is essential for scalability. This means breaking down complex systems into lower, independent modules that can be fluently integrated, modified and expanded without dismembering the overall armature. This approach promotes law exercise, reduces development time, and simplifies conservation as your incipiency grows.

Data-Driven Decision-Making

Embracing a culture of data-driven decision- timber is pivotal for navigating the complications of growth. By using data analytics, you can gain precious perceptivity into client geste, request trends, and functional performance, enabling informed opinions that drive strategic growth and optimize resource allocation.

Talent Acquisition and Retention

Investing in attracting, developing, and retaining top gifts is an essential element of a scalable foundation. A professed and adaptable platoon is the driving force behind invention, effectiveness, and the capability to acclimatize to changing demands. erecting a strong gift channel and fostering a culture of nonstop literacy ensures that your incipiency has the mortal capital to power its growth trip.

Process Robotization and Optimization

Automating repetitious tasks and streamlining processes can significantly enhance effectiveness, reduce costs, and free up precious time and coffers for strategic enterprise. Identify areas where robotization can streamline workflows, exclude redundancies, and ameliorate overall productivity, enabling your incipiency to handle increased volume without immolating quality or client experience.

Financial Planning and Vaticinating

Accurate fiscal planning and soothsaying are essential for fueling growth while maintaining fiscal stability. Develop comprehensive fiscal models that incorporate profit protrusions, expenditure vaticinations, and cash inflow statements to assess your incipiency's fiscal health and companion strategic opinions. This visionary approach ensures that your incipiency has the necessary coffers to support its growth bourns.

Strategies for Erecting a Scalable Foundation

Identify Growth Areas

Conduct thorough request analysis, contender assessments, and client feedback to identify implicit growth openings that will drive your incipiency's expansion. Understanding your request geography and target followership provides precious perceptivity into the direction of your scalable foundation.

Design for Scalability

Incorporate scalability principles from the onset of your product and system design. Consider factors similar to data growth, stoner business, and point expansion when making design opinions. This visionary approach ensures that your foundation is erected to accommodate unborn growth without expensive overhauls or performance backups.

Embrace pall- Grounded results

influence pall- grounded structure and services to gain inflexibility, scalability, and cost-effectiveness in managing your technology mound. pall results give on-demand coffers, elastic scalability, and reduced outspoken costs, making them well-suited for startups that anticipate growth.

Foster a Culture of Innovation

Encourage trial, creativity, and nonstop enhancement within your platoon. Foster a culture that embraces change, values learning from failures, and encourages invention in processes, products, and services. This mindset is essential for conforming to evolving request demands and maintaining a competitive edge in the face of growth.

Examiner and acclimatize

Continuously cover your incipiency's performance, identify areas for enhancement, and acclimatize your scalable foundation as your requirements and request conditions evolve. Regular performance reviews, data analysis, and client feedback give precious perceptivity for optimizing your systems, processes, and strategies to support sustainable growth. Erecting a scalable foundation isn't a one-time event; it's an ongoing process that requires nonstop attention, adaption, and a commitment to invention. By bedding scalability principles into your incipiency's DNA,

CHAPTER FOUR

SUSTAINING MOMENTUM: NAVIGATING THE PATH TO BREAKTHROUGH SUCCESS

In the dynamic and ever-evolving world of business, achieving breakthrough success isn't simply about reaching a peak of performance but rather about maintaining that instigation, prostrating challenges, and continuously pushing the boundaries of what is possible. Sustaining instigation requires a delicate balance between strategic planning, unwavering adaptability, and a deep-seated belief in the eventuality of nonstop growth. It's about navigating the ineluctable hurdles that arise along the way, conforming to changing request conditions, and arising stronger from lapses.

The substance of Sustained instigation

Sustained instigation isn't about maintaining the status quo; it's about continuously evolving, conforming, and instituting. It's about feting that success isn't a destination but an ongoing trip, where the pursuit of excellence nowadays ceases. At the heart of sustained instigation lies a grim pursuit of enhancement, the ability to challenge the status quo, and a commitment to embracing change.

The Pillars of Sustained Instigation

Strategic Planning and Adaptability: A clear and adaptable strategic plan serves as a roadmap for guiding the company's direction, aligning coffers, and navigating changing request dynamics. It provides a frame for making informed opinions, prioritizing enterprise, and conforming to unlooked-for challenges.

nonstop Innovation: is the lifeblood of sustained instigation. Fostering a culture of nonstop invention enables companies to identify new growth openings, disrupt traditional requests, and stay ahead of the competition. This culture encourages trial, embraces unconventional thinking, and celebrates creative problem-solving.

Empowering People and Teamwork: A company's success is eventually driven by its people. Empowering workers to contribute their ideas, fostering strong cooperation, and creating a positive work terrain is crucial to unleashing the collaborative power of the pool. When individuals feel valued, engaged, and empowered, they become catalysts for invention and growth.

Adaptability and Growth Mindset: Sustained instigation isn't a smooth, continued trip; it's a path marked by challenges and lapses. Embracing adaptability, learning from lapses, and espousing a growth mindset is pivotal for prostrating obstacles and maintaining instigation. A growth mindset views challenges as openings for literacy and enhancement, rather than invincible roadblocks.

Data-Driven Decision-Making: Data is the currency of the digital age. using data and analytics to gain perceptivity into client geste, request trends, and functional performance enables informed decision- timber and drives nonstop enhancement. By assaying data effectively, companies can identify areas for optimization, make strategic adaptations, and stay ahead of the wind.

Strategies for Sustaining Momentum

Embrace nonstop enhancement: and apply a culture of nonstop enhancement, regularly assessing processes, relating areas for enhancement, and making data-driven changes to enhance effectiveness and effectiveness. This ongoing pursuit of excellence ensures that the company remains nimble, adaptable, and responsive to changing requirements.

Invest in Talent Development: Invest in training, development, and upskilling programs for workers to ensure they have the chops and knowledge to acclimatize to changing requirements and contribute to invention. By investing in its mortal capital, the company empowers its pool to become motorists of growth and invention.

Monitor Market Trends and acclimatize: Continuously cover request trends, contender conditioning, and arising technologies to identify implicit pitfalls and openings, conforming strategies as demanded to maintain a competitive edge. This visionary approach ensures that the company stays ahead of the wind and seizes new openings.

Nurture client connections: Prioritize client connections by understanding client requirements, furnishing exceptional client service, and continuously perfecting the client experience. Building strong client connections fosters fidelity, reprise business, and positive word-of-mouth, which are essential for sustained growth.

Celebrate Successes and Learn from Setbacks: Fete and celebrate successes to boost morale and provocation, while also assaying lapses to identify areas for enhancement and make adaptability. This approach fosters a culture of literacy, growth, and nonstop enhancement.

Case Studies of Sustained Instigation

multitudinous companies have demonstrated remarkable success in sustaining instigation and achieving breakthrough success over time

Amazon's: E-commerce mammoth has continuously founded and expanded its immolations, transforming from an online bookstore into a global leader in pall computing, digital entertainment, and logistics. Amazon's unvarying commitment to client satisfaction, nonstop invention, and data-driven decision- timber has been necessary for its sustained growth and success.

Apple: The technology mammoth has constantly readdressed particular computing, smartphones, and wearable biases, maintaining its position as a leading inventor and trendsetter.

Apple's focus on design, stoner experience, and flawless integration across its product ecosystem has been crucial to its capability to maintain instigation and attract pious guests.

Google: The Hunt Machine colonist has expanded its reach into colorful sectors, including pall computing, online advertising, and artificial intelligence, establishing

Engaging customers and creating a sense of belonging where client preferences and prospects are constantly evolving, engaging guests and creating a sense of belonging is more pivotal than ever. By fostering meaningful connections with their guests, businesses can transfigure occasional buyers into pious lawyers, driving sustainable growth and brand fidelity.

The Significance of Client Engagement and Belonging

Engaging guests and fostering a sense of belonging offers a multitude of benefits for businesses

Enhanced client fidelity Engaged guests are more likely to come pious reprise guests, reducing churn and adding the continuance value of each client. fidelity programs and substantiated gests further strengthen client bonds.

Positive Word-of-Mouth Marketing Engaged and pious guests come brand lawyers, spreading positive word-of-mouth recommendations, attracting new guests, and enhancing brand character. Social media platforms and client communities amplify these positive voices.

Valuable client perceptivity Engaged guests give precious feedback and perceptivity, helping businesses understand their requirements, preferences, and pain points, leading to advanced products, services, and guests. Client feedback circles foster nonstop invention.

Increased client Continuance Value Engaged guests are more likely to make reprise purchases, purchase advanced-priced particulars, and try new innovations, contributing to increased profit and profitability. individualized recommendations and targeted marketing juggernauts maximize client continuance value.

Enhanced Competitive Edge A strong client engagement strategy can give a significant competitive edge, securing the business from challengers and attracting a pious client base. client-centricity becomes a strategic advantage.

Strategies for Engaging Guests and Creating a Sense of Belonging

individualized gests use data analytics and client relationship operation (CRM) systems to gain perceptivity into client preferences and geste. Deliver substantiated gests that reverberate with individual guests, acclimatizing dispatches, recommendations, and offers to their unique requirements and interests. use AI and machine literacy to enhance personalization.

Omnichannel Engagement gives a flawless and harmonious client experience across all touchpoints, including online, offline, and mobile channels. Integrate client data across platforms to ensure a unified client trip. Omnichannel marketing strategies produce a cohesive brand experience.

Community structure produces and fosters online and offline communities where guests can connect, partake guests, and interact with the brand. Encourage peer-to-peer relations, host events, and give exclusive benefits to community members. Online forums, social media groups, and in-person events foster a sense of belonging.

Interactive Content and Engagement produce engaging and interactive content, similar to quizzes, pates, contests, and social media juggernauts, to encourage client participation and commerce. Gamification and interactive gests enhance engagement.

Exceptional client service gives exceptional client service that goes beyond resolving issues. Anticipate client requirements, respond instantly to inquiries, and go the redundant afar to exceed prospects. Live converse, chatbots, and tone-service doors give 24/7 support.

Hand commission Empower workers to connect with guests in a particular position, furnishing exceptional service, addressing enterprises instantly, and fostering a sense of connection. Hand training and artistic enterprise inseminate a client-centric mindset.

Client feedback and Recognition laboriously seek and gather client feedback through checks, reviews, and social media relations. Use feedback to ameliorate products, services, and client guests. Fete and appreciate client fidelity through substantiated prices, exclusive offers, and special recognition programs. client appreciation programs foster strong client connections.

Erecting a Thriving Client Community

Engaging guests and creating a sense of belonging is an ongoing process that requires a deep understanding of client requirements, a commitment to substantiated gests, and a culture of client centricity. By enforcing these strategies and nurturing client connections, businesses can cultivate a thriving client community, transfigure occasional guests into passionate lawyers, and achieve sustainable growth in the digital age. Flashback, engaging guests isn't just about deals; it's about erecting a pious community that drives long-term success.

The Foundation of Success and Enduring Customer Relationships

The foundation of enduring success falsehoods in the capability to cultivate strong and continuing client connections. guests are the lifeblood of any association, and their satisfaction, fidelity, and trust are pivotal for long-term growth and profitability. structure enduring client connections isn't simply a transactional process; it's about creating an emotional connection, understanding client requirements, and furnishing exceptional guests that foster a sense of cooperation and collective respect.

The substance of Enduring client connections

Enduring client connections aren't erected on transitory trends or short-term earnings; they're embedded in a deep understanding of client requirements, a commitment to furnishing exceptional service, and a genuine desire to produce value for guests. These connections are characterized by

Trust and translucency

guests trust companies that are transparent in their communication, honest in their dealings, and responsible for their conduct. Trust is the foundation upon which enduring connections are erected.

Empathy and Understanding

Companies that demonstrate empathy and understanding of their guests' requirements, enterprises, and Bourne's are more likely to foster long-lasting connections. Empathy enables companies to connect with guests on a particular position and knitter their immolations consequently.

Exceptional client service

Exceptional client service isn't just about handling complaints efficiently; it's about exceeding client prospects, going the redundant afar, and creating memorable guests. Exceptional service leaves a lasting positive print on guests, making them more likely to return and endorse the company.

nonstop enhancement and Innovation

guests appreciate companies that are committed to nonstop enhancement and invention. They're more likely to remain pious to companies that constantly strive to enhance their products, services, and guests.

Open Communication and Feedback

Open communication and feedback circles are essential for erecting enduring client connections. Companies that laboriously seek and hear client feedback demonstrate their commitment to understanding and perfecting client gests.

Strategies for Cultivating Enduring Client Connections

Cultivating enduring client connections requires a strategic and harmonious approach. Companies can apply colorful strategies to foster fidelity and trust

Prioritize client- Centricity

Embed client-centricity into the company's culture and decision-making processes. Align all departments and workers with the thing of furnishing exceptional client gests.

Gather and dissect client Feedback

Regularly collect client feedback through checks, interviews, and social media relations. dissect feedback to identify areas for enhancement and address client enterprises instantly.

epitomize client relations

Use data analytics and client relationship operation (CRM) systems to epitomize relations with guests. Understand individual preferences and knitter dispatches consequently.

Empower workers to Deliver Excellence

Equip workers with the knowledge, chops, and tools they need to deliver exceptional client service. Empower them to resolve issues instantly and exceed client prospects.

Invest in Building Trust

Demonstrate translucency in business practices, be honest in dispatches, and fulfill pledges made to guests. Figure trust by being dependable, responsible, and ethical in all relations.

Show Appreciation and Fete fidelity

price client fidelity through fidelity programs, substantiated offers, and exclusive benefits. Show appreciation for client feedback and engagement.

produce a Community and Foster Engagement

Build a sense of community among guests by engaging them through social media, online forums, and events. Encourage client participation and feedback.

Case Studies of Enduring Client Relationship Excellence

multitudinous companies have demonstrated remarkable success in erecting enduring client connections and fostering fidelity

Amazon

Amazon's client-centric approach is apparent in its focus on furnishing exceptional client service, offering a vast selection of products, and constantly instituting to enhance the client experience.

Zappos

Zappos' emphasis on client happiness and furnishing exceptional service has earned it a cult- suchlike following among guests. The company's culture of empathy, translucency, and commission has been necessary for erecting enduring connections.

The Ritz- Carlton

The Ritz-Carlton's commitment to furnishing exceptional hospitality and exceeding client prospects has made it a symbol of luxury and individualized service. The company's focus on anticipating and addressing client requirements has fostered enduring fidelity.

Starbucks

Starbucks has converted the coffee experience by creating a welcoming atmosphere, offering high-quality products, and erecting particular connections with guests. The company's focus on creating a" third place" has cultivated a sense of community and fidelity.

Apple

Apple's client focus is apparent in its commitment to design, invention, and furnishing flawless stoner gests. The company's attention to detail and focus on creating products that guests love has fostered a strong following. Enduring client connections isn't a coexistence; they're the result of deliberate and harmonious trouble to produce value, foster trust, and exceed client prospects. Companies that prioritize client connections are more deposited for long-term growth, profitability, and sustainable success. By understanding the substance of enduring connections

CHAPTER FIVE

PLANNING FOR SUCCESSFUL EXITS AND SHAPING THE FUTURE OF ENTREPRENEURSHIP

achieving success isn't simply about launching an adventure but also about navigating its lifecycle effectively. While numerous entrepreneurs fantasize about long-term growth and sustainability, a significant portion of startups ultimately pursue exit strategies, seeking to monetize their sweat and pursue new openings. Planning for successful exits is an essential aspect of entrepreneurial success, as it allows authors to maximize the value of their gambles and pave the way for unborn trials.

The Significance of Exit Planning

Exit planning is a strategic process that involves relating and assessing implicit exit options, similar to accessions, combinations, original public immolations (IPOs), or operation buyouts. It entails precisely considering fiscal objects, request conditions, and the overall vision for the company's future. Effective exit planning can bring several benefits to entrepreneurs and their stakeholders

1. Monetization of Value

A successful exit allows entrepreneurs to realize the fiscal value they've created through their hard work and fidelity. They can reap the prices of their sweat and use the proceeds to fund new gambles, pursue particular pretensions, or give fiscal security to their families.

2. Attracting Investors and gift

Demonstrating a clear exit strategy can enhance a company's attractiveness to implicit investors and gifts. Investors are more likely to invest in companies with a well-defined path to monetization, while the top gift is drawn to associations with a clear vision for the future.

3. Strategic Inflexibility

Exit planning provides entrepreneurs with the inflexibility to make informed opinions about their company's future. They can assess colorful exit options, estimate implicit mates, and choose the strategy that stylishly aligns with their objects and the company's line.

4. Succession Planning

For entrepreneurs who ask to step down from their businesses at some point, exit planning facilitates a smooth transition of power and leadership. They can ensure that their companies continue to thrive under new stewardship, conserving the heritage they've erected.

Strategies for Successful Exit Planning

Start Early and Plan Proactively: Do not stay until the last nanosecond to consider exit strategies. Start planning to identify implicit openings, make connections with crucial assiduity players, and place the company for a successful exit.

Understanding your fiscal pretensions: easily defines your fiscal objectives for the exit. Consider factors similar to the asked valuation, duty counteraccusations, and the distribution of proceeds among shareholders and crucial stakeholders.

estimate colorful Exit Options: Research and estimate different exit strategies, similar to accessions, combinations, IPOs, and operation buyouts. Assess the pros and cons of each option in light of your fiscal pretensions, company's stage, and assiduity trends.

Seek Professional Guidance: Engage with educated counsels, similar to investment bankers, fiscal advisers, and legal counsel, to guide you through the exit planning process. Their moxie can help you navigate complex fiscal, legal, and duty considerations.

Stay Informed and acclimatize to Market Conditions: Continuously cover request trends, assiduity developments, and implicit exit openings. acclimatize your exit strategy as demanded to respond to changing request conditions and arising openings.

Shaping the Future of Entrepreneurship Fostering a Probative Ecosystem **

While exit planning is pivotal for individual entrepreneurs, it also plays a significant part in shaping the broader entrepreneurial ecosystem. A robust exit request can stimulate invention, attract investment, and encourage threat-taking, leading to a more vibrant and dynamic entrepreneurial geography.

To foster a probative entrepreneurial ecosystem that encourages successful exits and drives profitable growth, governments, assiduity associations, and educational institutions can play a vital part

1. Enhancing Exit openings

Governments and assiduity associations can foster a more favorable exit terrain by

- Promoting access to capital through colorful backing mechanisms, similar to adventure capital, angel investing, and government-backed loan programs.

- Easing combinations and accessions by connecting implicit acquirers with suitable targets and streamlining the nonsupervisory process.

- Creating duty impulses for successful exits, similar to reduced capital earnings levies or duty breaks for reinvesting proceeds into new gambles.

2. Supporting Entrepreneurship Education

- Educational institutions can incorporate exit planning into entrepreneurship classes, equipping aspiring entrepreneurs with the knowledge and chops to navigate the exit process effectively. This includes

- furnishing comprehensive courses on exit strategies, valuation methodologies, and concession ways.

- Organizing shops and forums featuring educated entrepreneurs who have successfully exited their gambles.

- Establishing mentorship programs connecting aspiring entrepreneurs with educated instructors who can guide them through the exit planning process.

3. Celebrating Success Stories

pressing successful exits and showcasing the achievements of entrepreneurs can inspire and motivate others to pursue their entrepreneurial Bourne's. This includes

Intimately feting successful exits through awards programs, media content marketing and branding have evolved far beyond traditional advertising and promotional juggernauts. They've come strategic imperatives that drive business growth, client fidelity, and long-term success. As businesses expand and reach a wider followership, the need to effectively gauge their marketing and branding sweats becomes decreasingly pivotal.

Scaling marketing and imprinting at scale requires a strategic approach that encompasses multiple angles

1. Defining a Clear and Compelling Brand Identity

Establishing a strong and harmonious brand identity is the foundation of effective marketing and imprinting at scale. A clear brand identity differentiates your company from challengers and resonates with your target followership. This includes developing a memorable brand name, totem, tagline, and brand voice that constantly represents your company's values, charge, and immolations.

2. Understanding Your Target Followership

Conducting thorough request exploration and followership analysis is essential for acclimatizing your marketing dispatches and strategies effectively. Gain a deep understanding of your target guests' demographics, psychographics, requirements, preferences, actions, and online habits. This will enable you to reach the right people with the right communication at the right time.

3. using Data and Analytics for perceptivity- Driven Marketing

Embrace data-driven decision-making by employing the power of analytics to measure the effectiveness of your marketing juggernauts and identify areas for enhancement. Track crucial performance pointers (KPIs) similar to website business, social media engagement, supereminent generation, conversion rates, and client continuance value (CLV). Use this perceptivity to optimize your strategies and maximize your marketing ROI (return on investment).

4. espousing a multi-channel Approach for Ubiquitous Reach

use a diversified marketing blend that encompasses colorful channels, similar to social media, search machine optimization (SEO), content marketing, dispatch marketing, paid advertising, influencer marketing, and public relations. Diversifying your channels ensures that you reach your target followership across multiple platforms and maximize your overall reach and impact.

5. Embracing robotization and Technology for effectiveness and Scale

apply marketing robotization tools and technologies to streamline processes, ameliorate effectiveness, and epitomize client gests. robotization can automate tasks similar to dispatch juggernauts, social media scheduling, lead nurturing, and client segmentation. This frees up marketing brigades to concentrate on further strategic enterprise, similar to creativity, content development, and crusade analysis.

6. Building connections with Influencers for Amplified Reach

Partner with applicable influencers in your assiduity to amplify your brand communication and reach wider followership. Choose influencers who align with your brand values, have a strong following among your target followership, and can produce engaging content that resonates with their followers.

7. Creating Engaging and Shareable Content for the witching liar

Produce high-quality, instructional, and engaging content that resonates with your target followership and encourages sharing. Diversify your content formats, including blog posts, infographics, vids, social media posts, and interactive tests, to feed to different preferences and engagement styles.

8. Measuring and Refining Strategies for nonstop enhancement

Continuously estimate the performance of your marketing juggernauts and upgrade your strategies grounded on data perceptivity and client feedback. Use analytics to identify what is working well and what needs enhancement, and make adaptations consequently to optimize your marketing ROI.

9. Prioritizing client Experience for Brand fidelity

Align your marketing sweats with your overall client experience strategy. ensure that your brand messaging, relations, and client service constantly reflect your brand values and produce positive client gests. This will foster client fidelity and encourage reprise business.

10. conforming to Evolving Trends and Technologies for Future Readiness

Stay acquainted with emerging marketing trends, technologies, and consumer geste patterns. acclimatize your strategies to influence new openings and ensure your brand remains applicable and engaging in the ever-changing digital geography. This includes exploring emerging technologies like artificial intelligence (AI), stoked reality(AR), and virtual reality(VR) to enhance client gests and produce innovative marketing juggernauts.

By enforcing these strategies, businesses can effectively gauge their marketing and branding sweats to achieve lesser reach, amplify their brand presence, and drive sustainable growth in the digital age. Flashback that marketing and branding aren't one-time enterprises but rather ongoing processes that bear nonstop refinement and adaption to remain effective in the dynamic business terrain.

Securing backing is frequently the lifeblood of a successful adventure. Whether you are an early-stage incipient or a seasoned entrepreneur seeking expansion, carrying the necessary capital is pivotal for transforming your ideas into reality and driving sustainable growth.

Navigating the Funding Landscape

The backing geography offers a different range of options, each acclimatized to specific stages of business development and threat biographies. Understanding these options and their felicity for your adventure is essential for making informed opinions and maximizing your chances of securing the right backing.

1. Bootstrapping Self-Funding for Early- Early-stage Gambles

Bootstrapping, also known as tone-backing, is a common approach for early-stage startups with limited access to external capital. It involves counting on particular savings, profit generated from original deals, or reinvesting gains to finance operations and growth. This approach offers entrepreneurs complete control over their business opinions and avoids the dilution of power associated with external backing. still, bootstrapping may limit the pace of growth and bear careful fiscal operation to ensure sustainability.

2. musketeers and Family Tapping into Personal Networks

musketeers and family frequently serve as early-stage investors, furnishing fiscal support grounded on particular connections and belief in the entrepreneur's vision. This backing option offers inflexibility and implicit benefits similar to reduced interest rates and favorable terms. still, it can be grueling to maintain neutrality and separate particular connections from business dealings.

3. Angel Investors Endured Entrepreneurs Backing New Ventures

Angel investors are individuals with high net worth who invest in early-stage companies in exchange for equity power. They frequently bring precious moxie, mentorship, and assiduity connections to the table, furnishing support beyond fiscal backing. Angel investors generally concentrate on gambles with high growth eventuality and the capability to induce significant returns.

4. Venture Capital Fueling High-Growth Implicit

Venture plutocrats (VCs) are professional investors who manage finances to invest in high-growth implicit startups. They generally give significant backing in exchange for a larger equity stake and laboriously share in the company's strategic direction. VCs are frequently picky and seek gambles with strong leadership, a clear request occasion, and the eventuality to disrupt diligence or produce new requests.

5. Business Loans Traditional Backing for Sustainable Growth

Business loans offer a more traditional form of backing, generally secured using collateral. They give access to a larger quantum of capital compared to bootstrapping or angel investors, but they also come with the obligation of repaying the loan with interest.

Business loans are suitable for established businesses with a proven track record and a clear path to profitability.

6. Government subventions and Programs on-Dilutive Funding openings

Government subventions and programs are given on dilutive backing openings for specific types of businesses or enterprises aligned with government precedence's. These subventions are frequently competitive and bear a strong offer demonstrating the impact and implicit benefits of the adventure.

Casting a Compelling Pitch Sundeck

Anyhow of the backing option you choose, a well-drafted pitch sundeck is essential to capture the attention of implicit investors and secure the necessary capital. Your pitch sundeck should compactly and persuasively communicate your business conception, target request, competitive analysis, fiscal protrusions, and growth strategy.

Negotiating Backing Agreements

Once you have secured backing offers, it's pivotal to precisely negotiate the terms of the backing agreement. Understand the counteraccusations of different equity stakes, vesting schedules, and liquidation preferences to ensure the terms align with your long-term business pretensions and the interests of all stakeholders.

Embracing the Backing Trip

Securing backing is an integral part of the entrepreneurial trip, furnishing the energy to transfigure your ideas into reality and drive your adventure's growth. By understanding the backing geography, casting a compelling pitch sundeck, and negotiating effectively, you can increase your chances of securing the right backing and embarking on a successful entrepreneurial trip.

CONCLUSION

The transition from incipiency to gauge-up represents a vital phase in the entrepreneurial trip, marking a period of rapid-fire growth, expanded reach, and the establishment of a sustainable business model. Navigating this transformative stage requires a mix of strategic planning, unwavering perseverance, and the capability to acclimatize to the ever-evolving demands of the request.

Throughout this comprehensive companion, we've excavated into the complications of the incipiency lifecycle, exploring the challenges and openings that arise at each stage. We've emphasized the significance of cultivating a positive and productive work terrain, attracting and retaining top gifts, engaging guests fostering a sense of belonging, and embracing nonstop literacy and growth.

crucial Takeaways for Scale-Up Success

Navigating the Startup Lifecycle Acknowledge and prepare for the distinct stages of the incipiency lifecycle, from creativity and founding to launching expansion, and implicit exit strategies. Understand the unique challenges and openings associated with each stage to make informed opinions and optimize growth.

Fostering a Thriving Workplace Cultivate a positive and productive work terrain that attracts and retains top gifts, energy invention, and drives sustainable growth. Encourage open communication, empower workers, promote work-life balance, and foster a culture of respect and addition.

erecting a Winning Team Assemble a platoon of passionate and professed individualities who partake in the company's vision and retain the reciprocal moxie necessary to navigate the scale-up phase. Attract top gifts through a compelling employer brand, competitive compensation, and a culture of nonstop literacy and development.

Engaging guests and Cultivating fidelity transfigure occasional guests into pious lawyers by furnishing substantiated gests, fostering an omnichannel approach, erecting communities, creating interactive content, offering exceptional client service, and laboriously seeking and valuing client feedback.

Embracing Nonstop Literacy and Rigidity The incipiency trip is a nonstop process of literacy, conforming, and evolving. Embrace challenges as openings for growth, stay informed about assiduity trends, and continually seek new knowledge and perceptivity.

Seeking Mentorship and Guidance influence the wisdom and experience of instructors, counsels, and assiduity experts to gain precious perceptivity, navigate challenges, and make informed opinions. share in incipiency communities and networks to connect with fellow entrepreneurs and seek support.

Celebrating Successes and Embracing Lapses Fete and celebrate mileposts, achievements, and platoon successes. Embrace lapses as learning openings, dissect the root causes, and pivot strategies as demanded.

Contributing to the Entrepreneurial Ecosystem Share knowledge, gest, and perceptivity with the broader entrepreneurial community. Support fellow entrepreneurs, tutor aspiring startups, and contribute to fostering a vibrant and probative entrepreneurial ecosystem.

The Transformative Power of Innovation and Resilience

The trip from incipiency to gauge-up is a remarkable testament to the transformative power of invention, adaptability, and entrepreneurial spirit. By embracing the challenges and openings that arise, continuously learning from gests, and contributing to the broader entrepreneurial ecosystem, scale-ups can play a vital part in shaping the future of diligence and driving sustainable profitable growth. Flashback, the scale-up phase isn't just about achieving fiscal success; it's about making a continuing impact on the world around you.

www.ingramcontent.com/pod-product-compliance
Lightning Source LLC
Chambersburg PA
CBHW062239290526
45794CB00006B/2343

* 9 7 9 8 8 7 0 7 4 4 3 1 5 *